AF261357

ENVELOPED IN LILAC HUES

ANDREANA WARLOW

Independently published 2022

ISBN: 978-1-7776740-5-2

"Give sorrow words; the grief that does not speak knits up the o-er wrought heart and bids it break."

William Shakespeare

We're changing seasons as the sun rises now before we do,
but it's unfulfilling
—I need the sun to shine in your eyes, too.
Sunday mornings are made for pottering around,
preparing plant beds for spring blooms.
Here, I'm a wreck, trying to hold my heavy heart up
with flowers in vases

to feel near you.

After the fall
after the fall

has been ruminating in my head.
I'm trying to make sense of it while
anxiously awaiting what's on the other end.
You know, I can be as still as a tree,
weathered by regular storms with emotions
unreadable for your eyes to see.
Yet once these bittersweet rains
I've been dreading crash down,
the wreckage will take a lifetime to mend.

After the fall,
I'm afraid of what's to be.

An eerily familiar feeling lingers in the air
pulling me/ prodding me/ holding me
hostage to despair.

Which way is up, and which way is out
when it's able to find you anywhere?

The fountain hasn't run dry;
there are far too many words still to be said.
I can tell by the way these tears overflow
each time my mind wanders, and
loving memories meet with regret.
Our hearts once beat in succession
as melodic as a ringtone.
Can we go back to when we'd end the chat with
"Please, call me when you get home"?

My body grew to house three
and inside yours,
I grew to know you.
Absorbed your thoughts,
memorized your laugh.
Time's ticking by way too fast
while I'm here, but
I'm not—I'm stuck, lost,
shuffling through tabs of thoughts.
Recollecting days gone in bird's eye:
we're on our way home from the park/
the moths are fluttering in after dark/
I've fallen and I can't let you know/
enveloped in lilac hues, you—without a doubt,
the one to keep me going.

I am forever grateful for your unwavering love
and support.
You are the strength running through my veins.

Tiny fissure cracks in all-consuming certainty.

Photos, words, and memories.
Forevermore, we'll be secured inside these.

And when you feel the emotions are too strong, or the aches are wearing you out or the weight is simply too much to bear—then stop, take a rest. My heart and arms are always open, come here.

The slowness of an early start on a brand-new day.
The weightlessness of a clear-sky morning filled with sweet
tunes as the sun rises.
The awareness that even after the darkest night, you've
made it through to see the light.

Keep on keeping on.

I hope you know I haven't forgotten you.
I need you to know I never will.

A dream within a dream within a dream
third-person view
laying down in the eye of the storm
I lost my place
but I've got a flag to raise
off-white
tainted by tears as my soul cried

I've tried, and I try
leaping bounds to get it right
then in comes the tide
and I'm back to running for my life
with my hands bound and tied
barefoot and aching
taking shelter within myself
holding the gentlest parts tight
to keep my sanity alive
because one day when I get it all right
the sun will seep into the cracks
and illuminate the darkest parts
I couldn't shelter from the hardest storms

Burning
Lit
Burnt out
Lights out

A fire sign burning out.
Fingers blistered and sore lighting matches
to keep the fire burning inside.
Spending time trying to figure out what's right.

Am I supposed to feel this way?
Am I losing time?

Sweet July,
you left me stunned.
I can't even tell you
how much I've cried
under your sweltering sun.

Even a tongue-tied with grief will
find the fortitude to speak if only
ever on to ears unwilling to hear
and hearts too stubborn to feel

There's a silence in the morning
between the rustling leaves
and the swift brisk breeze that's
too loud to ignore
and too deafening to escape.
It reminds me that every day
I'll rise again with heartache
that twists my insides no matter
how many steps I take.

Every day, every other,
we'd flow in and out of conversations
never skipping a beat.
Weaving intricate lines and staying connected
with what felt like a million miles in between.
I was yours and you were mine
without ever realizing what we'd
lose when we ran out of time.

Waves of change, most often paralyzing pains:
grieving a life that couldn't stay
and a life that paved the way.

Have the conversation you've been saving for the right time **now**.

I feel like I've been floating in and out of reality
and a lifetime of memories.
Trying to get a grasp on how life is going to be,
releasing my now foreign ideas
on how it was all supposed to be.

Rest here, peacefully

Allow yourself this time to deeply breathe

Recollect all your thoughts

Remember your life's dreams

Like the wind, you'll carry on, effortlessly

Just please, always know that
you won't be a forgotten memory
when you decide to go on your way
and set yourself free.

Into myself, I collapsed and folded.
Reconfigured my mind to shed the weight,
to see the light.

Have I said all I have to say

Pulled at every string and
unravelled my stagnant pain

It's true—for every question
I'll never get the answer

So, have I said all I really need to say

Has my soul searching been met with peace

Finally

Against my soul's urgency to be lifted,
it seems lately the sun's been shuddering
to kiss me as much as I need it to.
At the end of the day when my heart
is filled with pain and all my strength's drained,
the moon arouses me from gut-wrenching
vivid dreams—unable to reflect, the same as I,
too consumed by all the dark.

A reject from the sun's healing light

I used to dream I was falling.
Skydiving off a high rise
and just before I'd land,
I'd sit upright
heart beating out my chest with
too many questions bouncing around in my head.

I used to dream my teeth were crumbling.
Squeezing my jaw tight
and they'd pop out,
fall like rocks as
I'd move my tongue around
choking and screaming internally, horrifically.

Now when I sleep
I'm too tired to dream,
except when these visions come to me
of a love whom I long to see.
I resemble her and she flows through me;
I awake in sadness,
to spend the day clouded by grief
as they're the only places
I know we'll meet.

You feel the pull
You hear the calling
Release the reigns
Release the fear and
Lean into love

Ever stared at a word questioning its existence?
Racking your brain, wondering what tricks
your mind was up to today.
Surely, it's spelled that way but why
does it look so completely strange?

All these frames and albums house memories,
keepsakes for all the old days.
If I left it up to memory, we'd be playing
a losing game because those things fade.
Some days it's just "did it really happen that way?"

I meticulously study them and
feel the doubts wash away.
Scattered about are safe places we can always remain.

If only for another day.

It comes.
Albeit in waves
but nonetheless, it comes
and I can't shake or break the motions.
It's tiresome riding the rollercoaster of emotions.
It's hard not being washed away by the tides.
When it rains, it pours
and though I fear sometimes I'm not strong enough
to withstand the storms, I'll take comfort
in knowing that it's coming.
And it'll keep coming in any form, any day,
any way.

After all, these forms are only borrowed as well as our time. We're here to live, to love and then float on.

ABOUT THE AUTHOR

Andreana Warlow is a Canadian poet, author and creator.

ABOUT THE COLLECTION

Enveloped in Lilac Hues is a short collection of poems arranged in chronological order as written while processing and coping with grief. Raw words and thoughts trying to make sense of the pain to get through to the other side.

OTHER BOOKS BY THE AUTHOR

Wanderer and the Moon – a poetry and prose collection

www.AndreanaWarlow.ca
Instagram @AndreanaWrites